21st Century Legal C
By Richard L. Herm

Overview: Where the Jobs Are
The Hottest Attorney and JD-Advantage Opportunities

For additional booklet topics, updates, and legal career news visit http://legalcareerview.com.

21st Century Legal Career Series
Volume 4

Energy Law:
Fueling a Dynamic Legal Career

Richard L. Hermann

Published by H Watson Consulting LLC

To inquire about booking Richard L. Hermann to speak on 21st Century Legal Career Series content or other legal career management topics, contact donna@legalcareerview.com.

Cover design by Aaron Payne, aaron@awdience.com
Book design by Chris Rubio, info@thegeekfather.rocks

ISBN # 978-1-946228-06-2

To today's law students, who have many more career opportunities from which to choose than at any time in history.

Contents

About the Author

Richard L. Hermann graduated from Yale, the New School University, and Cornell Law School (following a stint in the U.S. Army, where he handled nuclear weapons and jumped out of airplanes). His first job out of law school was as an attorney at the Pentagon. He went on to work for the Government Accountability Office and Department of Energy. During his brief government career, he counseled friends and acquaintances on finding government law jobs, which evolved into launching Federal Reports Inc. The company became the leading provider of legal career information in the U.S. Among its many products were AttorneyJobs.com, LawStudentJobsOnline.com, and many other legal career publications and web products (all now the property of Thomson Reuters).

He also founded and led Nationwide Career Counseling for Attorneys and Sutherland Hermann Associates, an attorney outplacement and disability insurance consulting firm. Later he developed and taught the first law school course in *Legal Career Management* for online Concord Law School. He is also a regular columnist for *National Jurist*.

In the 1990s, he wrote three editions of *JD Preferred: 600+ Jobs You Can Do with a Law Degree (Other Than Practice Law)*. Today that number is 1,000+.

Legal Career View (http://legalcareerview.com) is Hermann's latest addition to his body of work on legal careers (both traditional and non-mainstream [a.k.a. "JD-Advantage]. *Legal*

Career View helps you connect the dots between today's news and tomorrow's jobs, shares Hermann's treasure trove of legal employment blogs, answers your questions, and provides strategies for securing a rewarding career in—and around—the law.

Richard Hermann's Recent Books:

Note: ABA books can be ordered at
http://shop.americanbar.org/ebus/store.aspx?term=Hermann

- *Manufacturing Business and the Law: A Guide to the Laws, Regulations, and Careers of the U.S. Manufacturing Revival* (American Bar Association [ABA], 2015). 758 pp. $129.95; ABA Member Price: $103.95
- *Practicing Law in Small-Town America* (ABA, 2012). 498 pp. $99.95; ABA Member Price: $79.95
- *Landing a Federal Legal Job: Finding Success in the U.S. Government Job Market* (ABA, 2011). 552 pp. $69.95; ABA Member Price: $54.95
- *Managing Your Legal Career: Best Practices for Creating the Career You Want* (finalist for Best Career Book, 2010) (AB, 2010). 424 pp. $69.95; ABA Member Price: $54.95
- *From Lemons to Lemonade in the New Legal Job Market: Winning Job-Search Strategies for Entry-Level Attorneys* (Decision Books, 2012). 254 pp. $30.00 from the National Association for Law Placement (http://nalp.org/bookstore).
- *The Lawyer's Guide to Job Security* (Kaplan Publishing, 2010). 240 pp. $28.31 from Amazon.com (http://amazon.com).

- *The Lawyer's Guide to Finding Success in Any Job Market* (Kaplan Publishing, 2009). 288 pp. $3.49 from Amazon.com (http://amazon.com) and BarnesandNoble.com (http://barnesandnoble.com).

Focus: What is This Booklet All About?

Energy law is a powerhouse practice area, one that will be a central focus of legal concern for as far out as the eye can see. That makes it a job-creating arena that aspiring attorneys should carefully consider.

Six factors have transformed energy law from a niche practice confined to a narrow geographic area into a wide-ranging endeavor that has gone global:

1. **Energy Independence.** The sudden emergence of the United States from 60 years of dangerous dependence on foreign oil imports from unstable regions such as the Middle East and Venezuela to the long-sought, and widely presumed, unachievable goal of energy independence is arguably the most important geopolitical event since the collapse of the Soviet Union.

2. **Technological Innovation.** Hydraulic fracturing ("fracking"), horizontal drilling, and "octopus" drilling made it cost-effective to produce oil and gas from deep underground deposits that were previously uneconomical to exploit.

3. **Relaxed Export Restrictions.** In 2015, Congress lifted the 40-year ban on oil exports, causing a rush by U.S. oil producers into world markets.

4. **Surging Natural Gas.** Fracking et al. made it cost-effective to substitute cleaner natural gas for coal and oil

in power plants and across many industries. It has also created thousands of attorney and JD-Advantage jobs.

5. **Nuclear Revival**. Construction of new nuclear reactors has been approved by the government for the first time in 30 years. Eight are planned.

6. **Rise of Renewables**. Clean energy is becoming more cost-competitive.

One of my first jobs after law school was as an antitrust attorney at the recently established U.S. Department of Energy (DOE) during the early days of the "Second Oil Shock," when Iran's Ayatollah Khomeini turned off the spigot and caused both U.S. gas lines to lengthen and the price of oil to skyrocket.

During my brief tenure at DOE, I was responsible for—

- Drafting regulations to govern the U.S. geothermal steam industry;
- Coordinating antitrust analyses of offshore oil and gas leasing policies with the Federal Trade Commission and Department of Justice;
- Determining the royalty amounts that major oil companies owed the government for offshore and onshore lease production;
- Developing transitional agreements with the U.S Department of Interior (DOI) concerning transfers of authority from DOI to DOE under the Department of Energy Enabling Act; and

- Reviewing and recommending contract awards for energy antitrust studies.

This was exciting stuff for a young lawyer. However, today's energy practice is light years more interesting and exciting than what I experienced. It is also very different. The issues that dominated back then are largely non-issues today. The geothermal steam industry, after years of dormancy, has awakened and is making slow but steady progress toward contributing to America's energy future. Outer Continental Shelf oil and gas leasing has slowed down and any antitrust issues have been shelved. The U.S. government still gets ripped off in terms of royalties from oil and gas leases because its accounting standards have not kept up with what is generally accepted in the rest of the economy. Turf battle disputes between DOE and DOI were settled years ago. And no one cares anymore about studying energy antitrust issues.

DOE's paramount concern back then and for the next three decades was energy independence and U.S. overreliance on oil imports from the volatile Middle East. Presidents Ford and Carter had instituted policies designed to lessen that dependence, consisting of tax incentives for energy conservation, strict automobile fuel economy standards, and examination of the viability of renewable energy sources. President Reagan, however, opposed those policies and overturned them, setting the stage for the next several decades of U.S. energy policy.

It was only the development of new drilling technologies in the 21st century that rendered concerns about energy independence moot. However, they did so at an environmental cost that has replaced dependence on Middle Eastern oil as one of the principal fears today.

The era of total neglect of a forward-looking energy policy is over. The Third Oil Shock (2008), when the cost of a barrel of Saudi Arabian Light Crude oil skyrocketed to over $140, then a few years later plummeted to under $40, demonstrated the harsh reality of what dwindling supply and increased demand can do...and undo. The Saudi refusal to limit production during and after the Great Recession, combined with the vexations of climate change, means that the U.S. and every other country can no longer continue their fossil fuel addiction.

This volatility and constant state of flux portend very good things for an energy law practice. Here's just one example of just how dynamic energy practice can be:

Hacking Into Supplies

Cyber hacking has become consistent front page news. However, if you think hackers are only stealing information, guess again.

There is a huge and thus far uncontained cyber security threat to energy companies, particularly oil and gas companies that ship their product to customers via pipelines. Digital monitoring combined with the "Internet of Things" (IoT) allows companies to remotely control the flow of their product through pipelines. While that is a great advance, it also opens up vast opportunities for both all of the usual players—oil, gas, and

8

pipeline companies—as well as criminals to manipulate the system and make it appear that the flow rates are something other than what they actually are. An infinitesimal change in what appears on the remote screen could mean millions of dollars' difference in who pays what amount to whom.

One place where something along these lines has already occurred is in the oil tanker industry. Russian hackers engaged by a shipper invaded a system that controls tank temperature and were able to decrease the temperature in the tank, thereby fitting more oil into the tank while reporting a smaller amount, and thus saving the shipper a lot of money.

There is probably a lot more of this going on than ever surfaces. Companies are loath to report hacking incidents because it jeopardizes their brand.

These technology combinations open up a whole new practice vista.

How Do We Know That Energy Law is "Hot?"

The fact that Energy Law is a hot practice area is not just a "gut feeling." Instead, it is based on a sophisticated practice area analysis that I developed over many years in order to be able to arrive at an educated conclusion about law practice areas and where they are trending. If you run Energy Law through the following 10 criteria that comprise this practice area analysis template, it emerges as a very hot field.

Note. It is not necessary that all 10 criteria be met for a practice area to be designated "hot." However, the more criteria that are met, the hotter the practice area. It is worth a legal job seeker's notice if a majority of the criteria are satisfied.

1. **Supply and Demand.** *Ideally, the demand for individuals who can do the work should exceed the supply of qualified individuals.*

    Three variables influence energy lawyer demand: (1) price; (2) geography; and (3) feedstock. When the benchmark price of oil is high or moving up, demand generally grows, and not only for oil industry attorneys. Conversely, when it is low or moving down, demand declines. While energy practice has expanded a great deal beyond its traditional boundaries— Washington, DC and the South/Southwestern "oil patch" states—there remains a geographic location constraint that affects demand (see criterion no. 5, below). Finally, the type of feedstock also affects demand. As energy practice differentiates itself depending on the specific energy source, e.g., oil, natural gas, coal, renewables, demand within an energy sector can vary considerably.

2. **Number of Job Opportunities.** *The practice area should offer a large number of job opportunities relative to other practice options.*

   The dramatic emergence of cost-effective extraction technologies such as fracking and horizontal drilling, along with the rise of renewables, has vastly expanded the number of energy legal job opportunities. This is particularly true of some of the JD-Advantage jobs discussed in this booklet.

3. **Sustainability.** *The practice area should not be a flash in the pan. It should exhibit signs that it will be around beyond the present.*

   Energy is one of life's essentials. We will be dependent on it as long as there is a human race.

4. **An Upward Curve.** *The practice area should be a growth industry.*

   Energy demand and use is directly proportional to population growth. Enough said.

5. **Geographic Scope.** *Jobs should be available nationwide, or at least in a large number of geographic locations.*

   The "oil patch" has expanded far beyond its traditional home in Texas, Oklahoma, Louisiana, Arkansas, and the Gulf of

Mexico. Today, 20 states have a robust fossil fuel industry due to the ability to extract oil and gas from previously unattainable formations at competitive costs. In addition, renewables such as solar, wind, and biofuels are closing in on a nationwide presence. In addition, energy has been a global practice for a long time and that is expanding, bolstered significantly by recent congressional action to lift a 40-year ban on oil exports.

6. **Relative Ease of Entry.** *The practice area's learning curve should not be too steep to be conquered by a novice. Some affordable education or training should be available to supplement basic legal education and experience.*

    While I can tell you from personal experience that the energy law learning curve is somewhat steep (learning a whole new "language" is part of it), there are plenty of opportunities to absorb what you need to know from both law school classes and certificate and comparable programs that ably supplement your JD (see *Breaking into Energy Law*).

7. **Ideally, It Should Be New or Different.** *The practice area should allow for opportunities for practitioners to be among those who are "first-past-the-post."*

    U.S. energy practice dates back to 1859 and, with respect to fossil fuels, is a "mature" practice area. Nevertheless, it can still surprise and throw new issues at practitioners. For example, the tension between the new drilling technologies and their environmental impact. Moreover, because energy law encompasses new energy sources such as renewables, there is always something new coming down the pike.

8. **Distinctive Value Proposition/Competitive Advantage.** *Practice area knowledge should be able to provide the elements of a unique selling proposition for a job campaign.*

   The more you understand about the energy industry and the myriad laws and regulations that govern it, the more value you bring to an employer. This is especially true if you grasp the substitutional nature of energy resources. Energy is one of those rare practice areas where both generalists and specialists can thrive.

9. **Threat Analysis.** *Is this practice potentially subject to substitution of a human lawyer by a disruptive technology...or something else? And how soon could this happen?*

   The folks who study the job futures market do not see a danger in robots or artificial intelligence replacing energy lawyers for a very long time to come, if ever. There is just too much judgment involved in the practice, much of it grounded in experience that cannot be "binaried" into data analytics. However, there is a danger down the road for oil and gas lawyers if renewables break through and replace fossil fuels, but that likely is a distant proposition. There is not much of a future today for attorneys who work in the coal industry.

10. Compensation. *Will this practice area allow someone to manage their student debt effectively?*

See *What Does It Pay?*

The Work

Energy law practice developed in response to U.S. government regulatory involvement in the creation, usage, sale, transmission, transportation, disposal and conservation of energy in all forms. Energy law, quite simply, deals with everything that is involved with exploration, development, distribution and pricing of energy resources. Today, there is a heavy emphasis on transactions, followed closely by regulation and litigation.

Energy law encompasses many practice areas, often with a unique twist. For example, acquiring real estate for oil and gas exploration and development might mean securing surface and subsurface rights, and competing for oil and gas tracts in government-run Outer Continental Shelf Lease Sale auctions.

For 100 years, the exclusive focus of energy law and practice was on fossil fuels: oil, coal, and natural gas. While that is slowly changing, politicians are at an impasse (hardly unusual in eternally gridlocked Washington, DC) over the development of renewable energy sources. Despite over a trillion dollars of wealth transfers to oil companies through the oil depletion allowance and other government largesse, renewables opponents are suddenly very vocal about the inappropriateness of "picking winners" in the battle for the energy future. The argument against renewables used to be that they were nowhere near price-competitive with oil. However, as prices have equalized, new arguments against renewables keep being raised, fueled by massive contributions from the oil lobby. The largest trade association in Washington, by a long shot, is the American Petroleum Institute.

However, holding back the rise of renewables is not a long-term strategy. Opponents are on the wrong side of history, never a winning tactic. Today, the increasingly prevailing mantra is that all energy resources (with the possible exception of coal) need to contribute to a national energy plan. Nothing is likely to be overlooked. Every possible energy alternative and technology will probably be pursued. That is very good news for attorneys interested in this practice area.

Energy practice is changing dramatically, attempting to keep pace with the massive policy changes necessitated by the rise of renewables, the decline of the coal industry, the problems caused by climate change, and the fact that the practice has gone national, no longer concentrated almost exclusively in Washington, DC and the oil patch.

Several major current developments directly affect legal careers in energy law (not in any particular order of importance):

1. Every time oil and gasoline prices surge, more energy law jobs are created.

- In 1973-74, the First Oil Shock caused prices to quadruple, eventually leading to the creation of DOE, the Federal Energy Regulatory Commission (FERC), and the Nuclear Regulatory Commission (NRC) which, in turn, led to the proliferation of a host of new energy practices in law firms of all sizes, boutique firms that focused exclusively on energy matters, and consulting firms that hired multidisciplinary professionals including attorneys.

- In 1979, the Second Oil Shock and its disruptions prompted another surge in hiring at federal and state energy regulatory and administrative agencies and, in response, in the private sector.
- In 2008, when the price of oil skyrocketed to $147 a barrel and the price of gas to more than $4 at the pump, hiring rose again in both the public and private sectors.

2. Drilling technology creates jobs. The new drilling technologies discussed above stimulated a tremendous hiring binge, this time throughout the U.S., especially in places with deep underground oil and gas shale deposits (in places like the Barnett, Marcellus, Utica, and Haynesville formations). This period was also marked by the largest increase in JD-Advantage energy jobs in history (more on that below).

3. Nuclear is back. In 2009, the NRC approved the first new nuclear reactors since the near-meltdown at Three Mile Island 30 years before. The NRC went on a hiring binge because certifying the eight new approved reactors is a tremendously complex and lengthy legal task. Again, the private sector response to this regulatory revival has been huge.

4. U.S. energy predominance. In 2014-15, the U.S. leapfrogged both Russia and Saudi Arabia to become the world's leading oil and gas producer. Despite the Saudi's

purposeful attempts to keep production high and prices low, and thus drive U.S. frackers out of business and regain the top spot in the oil game, lawyers keep getting hired.

5. Lifting of the oil export ban. Congress recently lifted the long-time ban on oil exports, thanks to our sudden energy independence. Attorneys are needed to negotiate and document the huge increase in international transactions.

6. Renewables are rapidly approaching price-competitiveness with oil. That has spurred the development of solar and wind energy and experimentation with such exotica as wave energy production and biomass.

7. The electric grid cries out for upgrading and evolution into the "smart grid."

8. Fracking regulation is creating jobs. This is primarily a state and local phenomenon since the Environmental Protection Agency has taken only baby steps toward federal regulation due to fear of hampering the hugely successful drive toward energy independence.

9. Climate change is creating jobs, albeit at a slower pace than the developments above due to political denial that a problem exists. The absence of the usual regulatory drivers of job creation that has informed so much of the surge in energy legal employment means that job

creation in this sphere is largely due to private sector initiatives such as Richard Branson's Carbon War Room (http://carbonwarroom.com) program.

Who Hires? "Mainstream Energy Law Jobs

21st century energy practice has expanded far beyond its traditional home among large law firms in Houston, Dallas, and Washington, DC. Today it can be found everywhere.

Private Practice

Private practice is the province primarily of large law firms and energy companies of all sizes. Law firms are leaping aboard the energy bandwagon with amazing speed. Almost every major U.S. law firm now has an energy law practice. Most try to be all things to all energy clients; others focus their attention on specific energy practice areas, such as utilities, oil and gas, clean coal technology (a non-starter thus far), alternative energy development, etc.

However, law firms of all sizes and even sole practitioners are finding an energy practice increasingly attractive, and the number of boutique firms that focus exclusively on energy law or one or two components of it is growing rapidly. Energy law is becoming so diversified that it is possible to concentrate a practice in niche areas differentiated by type of feedstock – oil, gas, coal, nuclear, wind, solar, biofuels, geothermal, waves, hydrogen etc. – and/or by type of legal expertise – transactional, litigation, regulatory.

The nature of energy resources and their utilization makes this an international practice, too. Many major law firms have both a domestic and international practice, as do multinational energy companies.

23

Corporations

The energy industry companies number in the thousands and include:

- Vertically-integrated oil companies (i.e., companies with operations spanning the entirety of energy industry activities from exploration, development, refining, and production all the way through to delivery of gasoline at the pump, such as Exxon-Mobil, Chevron-Texaco, and other Fortune 10, Fortune 500, and Fortune 1,000 firms. These firms have hundreds of attorneys positioned throughout their companies in general counsel, tax, compliance, procurement, and other offices.
- Companies that concentrate on one industry activity, such as exploration, production, refining, distribution, or retail.
- Pipeline companies.
- Utilities.

Because energy is one of the most heavily regulated businesses, companies of all sizes tend to have an in-house counsel office.

Venture capital firms are making significant energy industry investments, prompted by government and private interest in renewable fuels and energy efficiency technologies. They also employ attorneys or outside counsel with energy industry expertise to help them better understand their investments.

Public Sector Practice

Public sector energy practice is weighted heavily toward regulation (rulemaking, compliance, and enforcement) and industry stimulation through research and development grants and contracts. You might think that government energy practice is limited to DOE's General Counsel's Office. In fact, there are *more than 80 U.S. government law offices with an energy law practice*, 14 separate ones in DOE alone, as well as many other DOE offices where attorneys work in JD-Advantage positions. Other agencies with multiple law offices practicing energy law include: the Federal Energy Regulatory Commission, NRC, DOI, and the Department of Justice.

The proliferation of energy practices throughout the U.S. government is largely due to the number of congressional committees and subcommittees that demand a piece of the energy legislative and oversight pies. This is the result of the several energy crises that the U.S. suffered beginning in the mid-1970s, when suddenly energy became a top-of-the-fold national concern and an opportunity for heavy media coverage and political photo opportunities.

Every state government has at least one regulatory agency overseeing aspects of the energy industry. State agencies work on an extremely wide range of energy programs and policies, including:

- Energy efficiency in homes, buildings, industry and agriculture;
- Renewable energy, e.g., solar, wind, geothermal, biomass;
- Residential, commercial and institutional energy building codes;

- Transportation and heating fuel supplies, pricing and distribution;
- Oil, natural gas, electricity and other forms of energy production and distribution;
- Energy-environment integration (such as conservation to reduce air emissions);
- New and emerging high-efficiency transportation fuels and technologies;
- Energy security and emergency preparedness; and
- Many other energy matters.

Traditional energy producing states have more than one such agency, e.g., Texas —Railroad Commission, Attorney General Natural Resources Division, Coastal Coordination Council, General Land Office, Board of Professional Geoscientists, Lower Colorado River Authority, Public Utility Commission, Office of Public Utility Counsel. Every state also has a public service or public utility commission (see http://consumeraffairs.com/links/state_pucs.html for links to each state's utility regulator).

Nonprofit Organizations

The energy industry has spawned a large number of trade and professional associations and other nonprofits. Chief among these, in terms of the number of attorney and JD-Advantage job opportunities, are the associations. This group includes the following selection:

- Alliance to Save Energy (http://ase.org)

- American Association of Blacks in Energy (http://aabe.org)
- American Boiler Manufacturers Association (http://abma.com)
- American Chemical Society (http://acs.org)
- American Chemistry Council (http://americanchemistry.com)
- American Coal Council (http://americancoalcouncil.org)
- American Council for an Energy Efficient Economy (http://aceee.org)
- American Council on Renewable Energy (http://acore.org)
- American Fuel & Petrochemical Manufacturers (http://afpm.org)
- American Gas Association (http://aga.org)
- American Hydrogen Association (http://americanhydrogenassociation.org)
- American Lighting Association (http://americanlightingassoc.com)
- American Nuclear Society (http://ans.org)
- American Petroleum Institute (http://api.org)
- American Public Gas Association (http://apga.org)
- American Public Power Association (http://publicpower.org)
- American Solar Energy Society (http://ases.org)
- American Wind Energy Association (http://awea.org)
- Association of Edison Illuminating Companies (http://aeic.org)
- Association of Oil Pipe Lines (http://aopl.org)
- Association of Women in Energy (http://awenergy.net)
- Biomass Energy Research Association

(http://beraonline.org)
- Clean Energy States Alliance (http://cesa.org)
- Distributed Wind Energy Association (http://distributedwind.org)
- Edison Electric Institute (http://eei.org)
- Electric Drive Transportation Association (http://electricdrive.org)
- Electric Power Research Institute (http://epri.com)
- Fuel Cell & Hydrogen Energy Association (http://fchea.org)
- Geothermal Energy Association (http://geo-energy.org)
- Independent Petroleum Association of America (http://ipaa.org)
- Interstate Natural Gas Association of America (http://ingaa.org)
- National Association of Royalty Owners (http://naro-us.org)
- National Association of State Energy Officials (http://naseo.org)
- National Coal Council (http://nationalcoalcouncil.org)
- National Mining Association (http://nma.org)
- National Petroleum Council (http://npc.org)
- Natural Gas Supply Association (http://ngsa.org)
- Renewable Fuels Association (http://ethanolrfa.org)
- Smart Electric Power Alliance (http://solarelectricpower.org)
- Solar Energy Industries Association (http://seia.org)
- Sustainable Buildings Industry Council (http://nibs.org/?page=sbic)
- United States Energy Association (http://usea.org)

Some of these associations have law departments; all have government affairs departments, a large number of which are stocked with attorneys. In addition, attorneys can be found occupying both JD-Advantage and other association positions. Note that some of these organizations also list job opportunities on their websites.

The industry has also produced a growing number of advocacy and public interest organizations, many populated with law departments and/or attorneys. Note: Almost all such organizations have an "environmental bent." A selection follows:

- Clean Energy Group (http://cleanegroup.org)
- Earthjustice (http://earthjustice.org)
- Energy and Policy Institute (http://energyandpolicy.org)
- Environmental Defense Fund (http://edf.org)
- Environmental Law Institute (http://eli.org)
- Land Trust Alliance (http://landtrustalliance.org)
- National Association of Clean Air Agencies (http://4cleanair.org)
- Natural Resources Defense Council (http://nrdc.org)
- Union of Concerned Scientists (http://ucsusa.org)

International Agencies and Organizations

A number of international agencies maintain an energy law practice and hire American attorneys. They include:

- European Bank for Reconstruction and Development (http://ebrd.com)

- International Atomic Energy Agency (http://iaea.org)
- International Centre for Settlement of Investment Disputes (https://icsid.worldbank.org/en)
- International Energy Agency (http://iea.org)
- International Gas Union (http://igu.org)
- International Geothermal Association (http://geothermal-energy.org)
- World Energy Council (http://worldenergy.org)
- World LP Gas Association (http://wlpga.org)
- World Trade Organization (http://wto.org)

Who Hires? JD-Advantage Energy Jobs

In addition to generating a large number of positions for aspiring "mainstream" energy legal practitioners, the U.S. energy boom and embrace of renewables is creating law-related jobs. These are, at present, largely concentrated in areas where shale oil and especially natural gas reserves are abundant (i.e., North Dakota, East Texas, West Texas, Northern and Central Louisiana, Eastern Ohio, Central and Western Pennsylvania, Western Maryland and West Virginia), and states have not interposed bans on fracking (New York State, which has such a ban, sits on top of two of the largest shale deposits in the world).

While there is also a diversity of JD-Advantage opportunities resulting from the rise of renewable energy industries (especially wind and solar), the revival of nuclear reactor construction after a 30-year hiatus, and concerns about climate change, the number of such jobs is currently dwarfed by oil and gas opportunities.

JD-Advantage Job Titles

- Carbon Transactions Manager
- Compliance Enforcement Analyst
- Compliance Enforcement
- Analyst-Mitigation/Reporting
- Compliance Program Auditor
- Director of Nuclear Licensing
- Energy Advocate

- Energy Conservation Program Specialist
- Energy Efficiency Program Manager
- Energy Regulatory Affairs Professional
- Energy Trading Compliance Officer
- Landman (Oil and Gas)
- Land Agent
- Leasing Administrator
- Leasing Consultant
- Manager of Compliance
- Mineral Appeals Analyst
- Natural Resources Specialist
- Nuclear Regulatory Affairs Director
- Oil and Gas Leasing Policy Analyst
- Public Utilities Specialist
- Rate Analyst
- Regulatory Projects Manager
- Regulatory Representative
- Renewable Energy Program Specialist
- Right-of-Way Manager
- Transmission Right-of-Way Specialist
- Utility Contract Administration Analyst

A Word about Landman Jobs

The "Landman" job title deserves special attention because the number of these positions is so huge and growing. This position is found only in the energy industry, more specifically in oil and gas (and some coal). Between 2009 and 2014, which began with the Great Recession, more than 20,000 new Landman positions were created in Pennsylvania alone.

Moreover and most importantly, Landmen are frequently hired directly out of law school, based on their legal education alone, which the industry considers a big advantage. Another attractive feature about the job: you are not desk-bound all day, every day.

Landmen go out into the field to negotiate mineral leasing rights with landowners. They then document these transactions so that their company can explore for and develop these resources. Desk work consists of supervising and administering the resulting leases and royalty payments and answering legal and other questions.

The small size of most gas companies and recent discoveries of vast domestic gas deposits (more than 70,000 gas wells are currently being drilled in the Marcellus Formation stretching from Central New York southwest into West Virginia) make this a particularly favorable time to look for Landman jobs.

What Does It Pay?

Law Firms

Private energy practice compensation is comparable to other law firm and corporate practices. Major law firms typically start 1st-year associates at $160,000-$180,000 per year. Mid-size and smaller law firms pay less, and their compensation packages range all over the map, literally and with respect to where they are located.

Corporations

Corporate pay for entry-level lawyers is largely irrelevant to this discussion because Fortune 1,000 companies rarely hire recent grads without experience (several years are generally required). Experienced lawyers, however, can earn salaries and secure benefit packages that compare favorably to those of major law firms.

Landman Compensation

Landman salaries are high compared to many other professions, including a large chunk of the legal industry. Interestingly, they remained high even during the depths of the Great Recession. The average company landman salary in 2016 is approximately $135,000, with the median salary being approximately 119,000. Note: The average salary for an *independent* (freelance) landman is approximately $140,000; median salary: $100,000. A landman with a law degree can expect to earn around an additional $10,000 per year. Entry-level salaries range from approximately $60,000 to $80,000 per year. A landman with certification can expect that to add to annual compensation.

Government

Public sector agencies pay energy lawyers according to the same government pay scales that apply to other federal and state workers, with the U.S. Government at the top level (up to approximately $150,000 plus locality pay). Entry-level base salary ranges between approximately $42,000 and $67,000, depending on qualifications. Locality pay can add up to an additional 25 percent to base pay depending on location. Certain federal agencies, primarily those involved in financial regulation (e.g., Securities and Exchange Commission, Federal Reserve Board, Consumer Financial Protection Bureau, Federal Deposit Insurance Corporation, Office of the Comptroller of the Currency, Federal Housing Finance Agency, Freddie Mac, Fannie Mae) operate under a different and higher pay scale.

Nonprofits

Nonprofit pay ranges widely, with trade associations paying significantly more than public interest and advocacy organizations.

International Organizations

International agency pay scales generally apply across the board to all professional-level agency employees and, if located outside the U.S., often include an additional amount based on location and/or number of dependents.

As with all industries, practice areas and economic sectors, compensation also depends most often on size, employer location, and industry. The United Nations salary scale (https://careers.un.org/lbw/home.aspx?viewtype=SAL) is fairly typical.

Future Prospects

Historically, energy law and resulting employment has had its ups and downs due to the politicization of energy supplies. When the Saudis in 1973-74 and the Iranians in 1979 cut off the West's supplies because they hated Israel and disliked America, energy practices grew rapidly. When the political crises ended, they receded.

The 21st century, however, is different. Robust energy practices are here to stay. The increasing diversity of energy sources and supplies, U.S. energy independence, rapidly growing developing country demand, globalization, technological innovation, and the complexity of contemporary energy issues, have seen to that.

Some of the most dramatic changes to the industry, the ones that will affect energy law and practice the most, are specified below:

Coal

Coal is the one energy resource where the number of jobs, including attorney positions, is declining. The U.S. has enough coal reserves to fuel our economy for 800 years. But that comes with massive problems: extraction is a very dangerous undertaking; surface mining devastates the environment; and coal is a very dirty fuel.

"Clean coal" (the use of "scrubbers" to eliminate coal plant pollution, and coal gasification) is, to date, a myth. Scrubbers are not even remotely effective in minimizing air pollution, and coal gasification is too expensive at present (the price of a barrel of East Texas Light Crude would have to be around $300 a barrel for coal gasification to be economically viable). Utilities are converting power plants from reliance on coal to gas and biomass at a rapid rate. Sustained low natural gas prices and the environmental negatives associated with coal have driven these conversions. Currently, approximately 30 percent of U.S. power plants burn natural gas while 40 percent burn coal. The U.S. Energy Information Administration predicts that, by 2035, virtually every power plant will be burning natural gas.

Drill, Baby, Drill

There is a growing bipartisan consensus that we need to keep relying on fossil fuels, oil and gas in particular, for a long time to come. Even if renewables become cheaper than oil and gas, it will take many years for the necessary new infrastructure to come on stream.

Offshore drilling has been going on for 115 years, almost 60 years in the Gulf of Mexico. Its expansion to the offshore Atlantic, Pacific, and Arctic coasts will, in large part, depend upon demand.

A Boon to T. Boone

T. Boone Pickens, who barraged us for years with expensive TV ads about the need to cultivate our immense natural gas resources and switch our oil use to natural gas, has a good (medium-term) point in addition to a strong self-interest since he owns billions of dollars of gas reserves. There are already buses and cabs that run on natural gas. The problem is that there are only a handful of natural gas filling stations where you can gas up.

Flaring off natural gas from oil wells will stop. Natural gas is an immensely valuable resource and a linchpin of our energy independence effort. The U.S. has enough proven natural gas reserves (211 trillion cubic feet) to last us approximately 120 years at current usage levels. On an even more positive note, the volume of proven reserves is actually growing from year-to-year, thanks to new discoveries, a sharp contrast to shrinking global oil reserves.

What we need is the infrastructure to: (1) build or retrofit natural gas vehicles, and (2) provide incentives to the private sector to pepper the map with natural gas filling stations.

Fracking and horizontal drilling for natural gas will continue. Unlike oil, this extraction technology was only moderately affected by the Saudi production/price war that began in 2014. Natural gas' relatively clean nature means that it could become a significant substitute for powering vehicles of all sorts, including ships.

The threat to the technology comes in the form of the chemical and wastewater residue left by the fracking process, which can threaten water supplies, and increased seismic activity. Oklahoma, for example, has experienced an almost hundred-fold rise in the number of reported earthquakes since fracking operations in the state began.

To date, environmental legislation and regulations to prohibit or limit fracking have been almost exclusively a state initiative. The U.S. government, through the Environmental Protection Agency (EPA) and Bureau of Land Management (BLM), has taken only modest steps in this direction, and even these are now in limbo. In late June 2016, a Wyoming federal judge voided the Obama administration's fracking rules, writing that BLM lacks any authority to regulate fracking on public lands. He stated that Congress removed any such power in the Energy Policy Act of 2005. The decision also calls into question EPA's baby-step rules regarding fracking elsewhere.

Going Nuclear

The nuclear industry has been partially unleashed. The unfortunate overreaction to Three Mile Island (TMI) in 1979 was to slap a total freeze on building and licensing new reactors. Meanwhile, France went ahead and now gets over 75 percent of its electricity from nuclear energy (the U.S. gets 19 percent). Francois Hollande is not glowing in the dark. You don't need to run a dosimeter over the wine selection at your local retail outlet before you buy your bottle of 1982 Chateau Lafitte Rothschild.

The problem at TMI Reactor Unit 2 had nothing to do with an unsafe reactor. It started with a minor pump failure, which caused Unit 2 to overheat and the unrelated closing of two feedwater lines from the Susquehanna River designed to cool the reactor. This triggered two warning lights to go on in the control room, but the poorly designed control room panel – I am not making this up –*positioned the warning lights on the back of the panel*. Consequently, the control room staff did not notice that the feedwater lines had closed and a meltdown ensued. Instead of blaming the contractor who designed the panel and the TMI operating company who accepted such abysmal design work, we took it out on the entire nuclear energy concept. To our detriment.

Chernobyl should also be discounted. Unlike the Soviets, the U.S. has never built a reactor that lacked a lead containment shell.

The nuclear industry today is experiencing a turnaround. The NRC has approved eight new reactors and one is now almost operational. Consequently, nuclear industry hiring has moved into positive territory for the first time in a generation. The fact that nuclear power is one of the most heavily regulated industries means that it must hire more lawyers to keep it in compliance and represent it in rate and safety hearings.

Final argument: Many fewer people have suffered injury or death from nuclear power than from coal mining or oil drilling.

Café Au Lait

A centerpiece of today's energy policy is the "CAFÉ" standards, the fleet average gas mileage mandates that automakers must achieve by law. President Gerald Ford pushed the first CAFÉ standards through Congress in 1975 (they were then implemented by the Carter Administration). Unfortunately, the next four presidents and the Congresses with which they did battle did nothing to move this policy forward. In 2008, prompted by having to pay over $100 each time they filled up their Hummers, Congress reluctantly increased the CAFÉ requirements for the first time in 33 years. Since then, the Obama administration and Congress mandated even more stringent CAFÉ standards.

Understanding and implementing the standards requires a multidisciplinary approach by automakers that includes attorneys in the mix.

Alternative Energy

Alternatives to fossil fuels (a.k.a. "renewables") come in many forms. The biggest obstacles they must overcome are: cost competitiveness, vigorous opposition from fossil fuel lobbyists, massive campaign contributions from the oil and gas industry, and lack of infrastructure.

Accelerating demand for alternative energy, combined with cost reductions and tax incentives, means that "cleantech" companies are positioned to grow rapidly in the coming decade.

Since 2008, cleantech capacity worldwide saw more investment than new fossil fuel capacity.

Biofuels

Biofuels are combustible fuels created from recently living plants (in contrast, fossil fuels are formed by ancient plant matter that has been compressed into hydrocarbons over millions of years). Biofuels are most commonly liquids such as ethanol (an alcohol) and biodiesel (an oil) that substitute for gasoline, diesel, and jet fuel. Ethanol is formed by fermentation. Biodiesel is based on extracts of naturally occurring oils from plants and seeds and is burned in diesel engines.

Biofuels can also be solid fuels like wood pellets and biogas.

Ethanol feedstocks include corn (the primary feedstock) and sugar cane. Biodiesel, feedstocks are primarily soybean and canola oils. These "first-generation" biofuels are the easiest to break down. "Second-generation" biofuels are produced from cellulosic material such as wood, grasses, and inedible plant parts, materials more difficult to break down through fermentation and therefore more expensive. There is even a "third-generation" biofuel that uses lipid production from algae. In recent years, a fourth category, "advanced biofuels," uses waste such as garbage, animal fats, and spent cooking oil to produce liquid fuels.

Biofuels' big advantage is that it is the only technological and economic replacement for fossil-based transportation fuels, primarily because they can be used in existing internal combustion engines without altering engines and with only modest infrastructure changes. A second advantage is that the plants that produce them can be replenished very quickly, especially compared to the millions of years it takes for fossil fuel replenishment.

Their biggest downside is that their principal feedstocks are also food products, which means that their diversion to a fuel drives up food prices. Moreover, the subsidies that biofuels like ethanol receive from government have become a controversial political issue, as evidenced by the first-in-the-nation Iowa caucuses every four years. In addition, there are environmental concerns ranging from water depletion and fertilizer use to deforestation associated with the expansion of land devoted to farming.

Ethanol today accounts for approximately 10 percent of the fuel burned in America's vehicles. Ethanol is nice, but what it does to food prices is not. There is a lot of feedstock out there other than corn that can produce ethanol, and that will likely be the redirection of this element of energy policy moving forward. Cellulosic biomass such as agricultural residue, sawdust, dead trees, municipal solid waste, etc., are capable substitutes for corn and have no bearing on food production or prices. The problem, however, is cost. Consequently, many pilot projects have either stalled or shut down.

Biofuels are not going to go away. However, you need to be careful if you want to practice in this alternative energy field. A focus on them has become one element in state and local economic development strategies, especially those that focus on business attraction and job creation. Northeast Ohio, especially the area around Cleveland and Cuyahoga and neighboring counties, is an example of this strategy.

Solar

Solar power research and development was in its early stages, but moving along quite nicely when, on January 21, 1981, it was essentially shelved. At the time, the U.S. government had been doling out a small amount of money ($30 million) to General Electric and a few other companies to experiment with solar technologies. Then ideology intervened ("government should not be in the business of picking winners") and the research came to a screeching halt. U.S. solar power development basically had to scrounge for R & D money for the next generation.

That has changed in the last decade. Solar energy is expected to grow by more than 600 percent between 2010 and 2020.

Wind

Wind, which is actually a form of solar energy (I'll spare you the scientific explanation) is one of the most abundant energy sources on the planet. An average onshore wind turbine produces more than 6 million kilowatt hours per year, enough to supply 1,500 households with electricity. At this writing, there are over 48,800 wind turbines producing almost 75,000 megawatts in 40 states. More than 500 wind manufacturing facilities operate in 43 states.

However, wind's development has been slowed by a combination of (1) high development costs, (2) the absence of a delivery system to get the electricity wind farms produce to the electrical grid and subsequently to consumers, and (3) intense lobbying against federal subsidies by fossil fuel industries. Nevertheless, wind energy facilities are expected to increase by almost 300 percent by 2020.

Development costs have come down to where wind energy is close to being cost-competitive with fossil fuels. Connectivity to the grid is slowly happening, thanks in large part to the stimulus provided by the American Recovery and Reinvestment Act (a.k.a. the Stimulus Bill). Congress has also grudgingly extended modest wind subsidies for ten years.

Wind energy is abundant in many parts of the U.S. states, i.e., places which have an average annual wind speed of at least 13 miles per hour. A useful resource for legal job-seekers who want to identify wind energy industry concentrations (i.e., where the jobs are likely to be) is the *United States Wind Resource Map* (http://windeis.anl.gov/guide/maps/map2.html).

Also watch for offshore wind farm development in shallow ocean and Great Lakes regions, where there is always a lot more wind than onshore.

Wave and Tidal Energy

Waves are produced by wind blowing across the ocean surface, which makes them yet another solar energy derivative. Tides, a form of wave power, are produced by the pull of the moon on the earth.

Water is about 800 times denser than air. Consequently, wave energy density exceeds that of wind by many orders of magnitude, greatly increasing the amount of available energy available. Waves can also be predicted days in advance. Tides are totally predictable.

One major problem preventing the rapid development of wave energy is that waves are too powerful and produce *too much* energy.

Some years ago, I hitched a ride to Miami from a conference in Ft. Lauderdale with a gentleman who was on his way to Florida Power and Light to pitch the utility on his wave energy device. I pored over his blueprints during the ride and concluded that he was certifiable (underscored by his passing slower vehicles on the shoulder). Not anymore.

Wave energy is the most concentrated and least variable form of renewable energy. The World Energy Council says that wave energy could become the lowest cost renewable energy source, and that it has the potential to produce approximately 2 terawatts (2 million megawatts), double current world electricity production.

Buoys, turbines, and other technologies can capture waves and tides and convert them into clean electricity. Like other renewables, waves and tides are variable.

Capturing wave power can be used to generate electricity, for water desalination, and for pumping water into reservoirs.

Wave energy technology has improved considerably and has tested as viable in recent experiments. Both the U.S. Navy and Department of Energy are awarding contracts to test the concept. However, the U.S. is far behind Canada and the UK in developing this energy source.

There are a lot of waves out there.

The Hydrogen Economy

Hydrogen is the "wave" of the future. The universe is loaded with it. The Sun burns 11 billion pounds of hydrogen *every second*. It is by far the most abundant element on Earth. If we can convert to hydrogen power, we can replace fossil fuels and every other energy source altogether.

Hydrogen plants do nothing more complicated than split water molecules into hydrogen and oxygen through electrolysis. The only problem is that, at current costs, it cannot compete with oil. It costs far too much in electricity costs to produce a gallon of hydrogen. Right now it costs more than twice as much per mile to drive Toyota's hydrogen-fueled Mirai than it costs to drive a gasoline-fueled car.

But this does not mean that we are not pouring research dollars into making hydrogen more efficient and safe (remember the *Hindenburg*). Both the U.S. Department of Energy and the government's National Renewable Energy Laboratory are funding multiple hydrogen fuel projects.

Geothermal

Geothermal technology has come a long way in 50 years, but is largely economically viable only in places like Iceland, where you cannot walk down the streets and rural footpaths without getting your behind singed by a thermal vent. Nevertheless, there is a role for geothermal, primarily in heating homes and buildings.

Geothermal energy derives from the heat produced by the Earth. The upper 10 feet of the Earth's surface has a steady temperature between 50° and 60°F. Geothermal heat pumps that pull up this heat can heat and cool buildings, provide hot water, and grow plants in greenhouses, among other uses. Geothermal heat pump systems consist of a heat pump, ductwork, and a system of pipes buried in the ground near the building.

The primary U.S. geothermal reservoirs are located in the West, Alaska, and Hawaii.

Geothermal costs now border on becoming competitive with fossil fuels.

By far the most enticing geothermal potential lies much farther below the Earth's surface. Hot dry rocks lie 3 to 5 miles everywhere beneath the surface. The technology to exploit this immense resource—injecting cold water down one well, circulating it through hot rock, and extracting the heated water from another well, is thus far much too expensive to be feasible.

Hydropower

The assumption is that we have maximized what we can do with this technology. Not true. There is a lot of moving water in the U.S. that has not yet been exploited. Our successful experience with massive projects like the Tennessee Valley Authority, Boulder Dam, and the Grand Coulee Dam is being re-examined for application to sites that have not yet been harnessed. There are a lot of them and this is cheap, constantly replenishing energy.

Breaking into Energy Law

Launching or reinventing yourself as an energy lawyer is not difficult. Since energy law is heavily transaction and regulation-oriented, any attorney at any career stage should be able to function and succeed as an energy lawyer.

The fact that so much of energy law is developing and evolving as we speak also makes this a practice area that does not require much prior experience. Renewable energy resources, for example, are just now emerging as a key component of energy law practice.

Thanks to the new technologies that make deep shale oil and gas viable, and the move toward renewables, there is a big demand for energy lawyers. Law firms engage in bidding wars for experienced energy attorneys. There is also a "trickle-down" effect in play, wherein energy practices are expanding and seeking new recruits.

Supplementing Your Law Degree

Credential enhancements can be both useful in terms of increasing your knowledge of the field and making you a more attractive candidate, as well as accelerating promotions.

Selected credentialing programs include:

- University of Vermont Law School (http://vermontlaw.edu)

- Master of Energy Regulation and Law (open to JD candidates from other law schools)
- Thunderbird Online (http://online.thunderbird.edu/certificate-oil-gas-management)
  - Online Certificate in Global Oil & Gas Management
- OECD—Nuclear Energy Agency (http://nea.fr)
  - International Nuclear Law Essentials (5-day course offered in February)
- Stanford University (http://academicearth.org/universities/stanford)
  - Energy Seminar (online)[A free, 15-lecture course]
  - Energy Innovation and Emerging Technologies Certificate (http://scpd.stanford.edu)
- Marylhurst University (http://onlinedegrees.marylhurst.edu)
  - Accelerated Online MBA in Sustainable Business: Concentration in Renewable Energy (online)
- Penn State Online (http://worldcampus.psu.edu/degrees-and-certificates/wind-energy-certificate/overview)
  - Graduate Certificate in Wind Energy
- Texas Tech University (https://depts.ttu.edu/elearning/certificate/wind-energy)
  - Wind Energy Certificate Program (online)
- New York University School of Professional Studies (http://scps.nyu.edu)
  - Graduate Certificate in Global Energy
- University of Denver, Sturm College of Law (http://law.du.edu)

- LL.M. in Environmental and Natural Resources Law and Policy
  - Certificate of Studies (CS) in Natural Resources Law and Policy
- University of Houston Law Center (http://law.uh.edu/eenrcenter)
  - LLM Program in Energy, Environment and Natural Resources Law
- American Association of Professional Landmen (http://landman.org)
  - Certified Professional Landman
  - Registered Professional Landman Designation
  - Registered Landman Designation
- University of Nevada-Reno (http://unr.edu/degrees/renewable-energy/certificate)
  - Graduate Renewable Energy Certificate (online)

Note. Neither LLM nor certificate programs are ever "locked in concrete." They appear and disappear frequently, usually due to two factors: (1) a hot new area that looks to be profitable for the offering institution; and (2) lack of interest in the program by prospective students.

Program Due Diligence

You need to do a thorough due diligence investigation of any supplemental program, whether an LLM or other Master's-level degree, or a certificate before you enroll and write a check.

Due diligence in this case consists of talking to individuals who know a lot about the program and its value. Make sure you speak with the following people:

Individuals who have already earned the credential. Get their opinions as to whether the credential made a difference to their careers, employability, promotion potential and compensation. Ask them:

- How difficult was it to find suitable employment after completing the program?
- How much help – and what kind of help – did they receive with respect to finding employment from the granting institution's career and/or program office?
- Would they do it again?

Employers of individuals who have recently earned the credential. Ask them:

- Do they value the fact that their employee has the credential?
- Would they have hired the employee absent the credential?
- How does the credential benefit their organization?
- Do they believe the credential is truly a career booster?
- What is their opinion of the credential-granting organization?

Current students in the program. Ask them:

- Is the program worth their time, effort, money, and career interruption?
- What do they intend to do with their degree or certificate?
- How much and what is the nature of the career assistance they are receiving from the granting institution?

Career placement professionals and/or program directors at the sponsoring school or other provider organization. Ask them:

- Where can you expect to work once you successfully complete the program?
- What is the institution's track record when it comes to placing program graduates?
- Where do recent graduates work and what career paths will be open to you armed with the credential?
- What specific job-hunting assistance do they provide both during and after you complete the program?

If they "stone-wall" you, state that they do not maintain such information or statistics, assert privacy or confidentiality reasons for not sharing this information, or become defensive, or if their answers are vague or otherwise unsatisfactory, say "thank you," pocket your check or loan application, and walk away.

Membership Organizations

The following selected membership organizations are excellent networking, educational, informational, and early job opportunity alert resources for anyone interested in an energy law career. A number of them have local chapters around the country. Several list job opportunities on their websites. Membership organizations are also superb resources for identifying and targeting specific employers.

- Alliance to Save Energy (http://ase.org)
- American Bar Association – Section of Environment, Energy & Resources (http://americanbar.org/groups/environment_energy_resources.html)
- American Bar Association – Renewable, Alternative and Distributed Energy Resources Committee (http://apps.americanbar.org/dch/committee.cfm?com=NR252300)
- American Bar Association – Section of Public Utility, Communications and Transportation Law (http://americanbar.org/groups/public_utility.html)
- American Council On Renewable Energy (http://acore.org)
- Association of Energy Services Professionals (http://aesp.org)
- Energy Bar Association (http://eba-net.org)
- Federal Bar Association – Environment, Energy & Natural Resources Law Section (http://fedbar.org)
- Institute for Energy Law (http://cailaw.org/institute-for-energy-law/index.html)
- Natural Resources Defense Council (http://nrdc.org)

Know the Industry

My friend Mike, an attorney in Washington state, *never* loses a client. Why? Because when he secures a new client, the first thing he does is immerse himself in the client's business. For example, when he was initially engaged by a manufacturing firm that produced telephone poles, he (1) immediately went out with the loggers to learn which trees were "pole-appropriate," (2) spent a day at his client's factory observing the process that transforms trees into telephone poles, (3) "shadowed" a sales representative as he visited prospective buyers, and (4) went out with an unrelated company and watched them replace decayed poles with new ones. Mike's clients are always dazzled by his interest, enthusiasm, and knowledge of their businesses.

If you want to make an impression on prospective employers and distinguish yourself from your job competitors, do what Mike does and learn as much as you can about what they do and how they do it. Practice area and industry knowledge are invaluable and pay off in job offers, status, promotions, remuneration, and job security.

This is particularly true with respect to the energy industry, with its highly unique business models (e.g., vertically-integrated oil companies), corporate structures (e.g., oil and gas exploration partnerships), relationships among "substitution" fuels, distribution channels (e.g., the grid, distributive vs. centralized), regulatory regimes, royalty arrangements, and nomenclature (e.g., BTUs, octopus drilling, etc.). If you want to impress employers with your knowledge, foresight in preparing for interviews and work, and the "sweat equity" you put in learning about what they do, and imprint yourself on them when hiring-decision time arrives, this is the way to accomplish that.

Finding Out About Jobs before Everyone Else

Being able to learn about job opportunities *before* they become public knowledge is an invaluable leg up on the competition. It enables you to get in line in front of your competitors by getting your application into the employer before anyone else, and often even before a job ad or vacancy announcement is published. When it comes to energy law, there are a variety of highly effective ways to do that:

Congressional appropriations subcommittee testimony. Every spring, top government agency officials go before Senate and House appropriations committees to explain in detail their budget requests for the next fiscal year. Often, they drill down into the particulars to the extent that they specify the number of new legal and law-related positions they seek. Testimony transcripts are typically available on committee websites.

When you read such testimony, keep in mind that even if it does not drill all the way down to specific numbers, you may find evidence of policy and regulatory initiatives and shifts that will alert you that additional lawyers might be required in order to implement these projects and programs.

Moreover, every such government initiative invariably leads to private sector responses that generate multiples of any new federal legal jobs.

Technology commercialization opportunities. Technological innovation frequently means new business for existing companies and even spawns new business startups. You can monitor this activity on a variety of government and university websites, e.g., the National Aeronautics and Space Administration (http://nasa.gov), the Federal Laboratory Consortium (http://federallabs.org), and the Association of University Technology Managers (http://autm.net).

Government Annual Performance Plans and Strategic Plans. These can also be mined for "hidden" job opportunities. Annual Performance Plans are, as their name indicates, prepared and published on department and agency websites each year. Strategic Plans are prepared and published on agency websites every 3-5 years. These legally-required documents are more "hit-or-miss" than Appropriations subcommittee testimony.

Federal budget documents. Examine the annual proposed *Budget of the United States*, best viewed at http://omb.gov. Forget about the actual budget itself, largely a collection of dizzying numerical data. Instead, examine each relevant department and agency's (e.g., Energy Department, Interior Department, Federal Energy Regulatory Commission) *Budget Appendix*, primarily textual documents that explain funding requests.

Take stock. Energy companies whose shares are steadily increasing in value (for non-speculative reasons) have a consistent history of hiring new employees, including attorneys.

Study financials. Become a consistent and careful reader of financial publications. Mainstream media and investment newsletters contain a great deal of this kind of advance information about where the legal and law-related jobs are likely to be in the near term.

Identify new financings. Newspaper business/financial sections and online financial websites often carry announcements of significant energy business financings. New financings usually predate major expansions and a corresponding need for additional employees.

Hunt for profits. Scan newspaper and online tables showing quarterly earnings reports for energy companies that have increased their profits by more than five percent from the preceding year. This growth rate often presages a need for additional employees.

Join energy law and related membership organizations. Like-minded professionals invariably band together to enhance their professional development and business and job opportunities. The energy community is no stranger to this and offers a variety of options for aspiring energy lawyers to "learn and earn." One of the most important things you can learn about at organization meetings is pending job opportunities. See *Breaking into Energy Law* for a list of such organizations.

Follow-Up

The sources of information listed below are organized by fuel feedstock. The last section lists a large number of general information resources

Alternative Energy (General)

- Alternative Energy News (http://alternative-energy-news.info)
- American Council for an Energy Efficient Economy (http://aceee.org)
- American Council on Renewable Energy (ACORE) (http://acore.org)
- Clean Energy States Alliance (http://cesa.org)
- Energy Planet Renewable Energy Directory (http://energyplanet.info)
- National Alternative Fuels Training Consortium (http://naftc.wvu.edu)
- Renewable Fuels Association (http://ethanolrfa.org)
- U.S. Green Building Council (http://usgbc.org)

Biofuels

- Biomass Magazine (http://biomassmagazine.com)

Coal

- American Coal Council (http://americancoalcouncil.org)
- National Mining Association (http://nma.org)

Electricity/Power

- Edison Electric Institute (http://eei.org)
- Electric Drive Transportation Association (http://electricdrive.org)
- Electric Power Research Institute (http://epri.com)
- Federal Energy Regulatory Commission (http://ferc.gov)
- Harvard Electric Policy Group (http://hks.harvard.edu/hepg)

Fuel Cells

- California Fuel Cell Partnership (http://cafcp.org)
- Hydrogen and Fuel Cells Interagency Working Group (http://hydrogen.gov)

Geothermal

- Geothermal Energy Association (http://geo-energy.org)
- Geothermal Resources Council (http://geothermal.org)
- International Geothermal Association (http://geothermal-energy.org)

Hydrogen

- American Hydrogen Association (http://clean-air.org)
- International Association for Hydrogen Energy (http://iahe.org)
- Fuel Cell and Hydrogen Energy Association (http://www.fchea.org)

Hydropower

- National Hydropower Association (http://hydro.org)
- U.S. Society on Dams (http://ussdams.org)
- International Hydropower Association (http://hydropower.org)

Nuclear

- International Atomic Energy Agency (http://iaea.org)
- Nuclear Energy Institute (http://nei.org)
- Nuclear Regulatory Commission (http://nrc.gov)

Oil and Gas

- American Gas Association (http://aga.org)
- American Petroleum Institute (http://api.org)
- Association of International Petroleum Negotiators (http://aipn.org)
- Association of Oil Pipe Lines (http://aopl.org)
- International Gas Union (http://igu.org)
- Interstate Natural Gas Association of America (http://ingaa.org)
- National Association of Royalty Owners (http://naro-us.org)
- Organization of Petroleum Exporting Countries (OPEC) (http://opec.org)
- Rocky Mountain Mineral Law Foundation (http://rmmlf.org)
- World Petroleum Congresses (http://world-petroleum.org)

Solar

- American Solar Energy Society (http://ases.org)
- Smart Electric Power Alliance (http://solarelectricpower.org)
- Solar Energy Industries Association (http://seia.org)

Wave

- Wave Energy Centre (http://wavec.org/en)

Wind

- American Wind Energy Association (http://awea.org)

General/Miscellaneous

- Association of State Energy Research and Technology Transfer Institutions (http://asertti.org)
- Energy Bar Association (http://eba-net.org)
- Energy Frontiers International (http://energyfrontiers.org)
- Energy Information Administration (http://eia.gov)
- European Bank for Reconstruction and Development (http://ebrd.com)
- International Centre for Settlement of Investment Disputes (http://worldbank.org/icsid)
- International Energy Agency (http://iea.org)
- Midwest Energy Association (http://midwestenergy.org)
- National Association of Manufacturers (http://nam.org)

- National Association of State Energy Officials (http://naseo.org)
- National Ocean Industries Association (http://noia.org)
- North American Development Bank (http://nadbank.org)
- United Nations Industrial Development Organization (UNIDO) (http://unido.org)
- United States Energy Association (http://usea.org)
- U.S. Department of Energy (http://energy.gov)
- U.S. Department of Interior (http://doi.gov)
- World Energy Council (http://worldenergy.org)
- World Trade Organization (http://wto.org)

21st Century Legal Career fields by their nature are constantly changing and responding to a variety of pressures including the political environment, technological innovation, globalization, etc. Updates from the author on the material contained in this booklet are posted at http://legalcareerview.com. *Find the new information for this title under the 21st Century Careers menu on the home page. Check the Updates link on that page frequently.*

Made in the USA
Columbia, SC
04 August 2019